EVERYBODY LIKES THE PIANO

T0039792

A Piano Course in Four Books

Composed, Arranged and Edited by

JOSEPH M. ESTELLA

CONTENTS

	Page
Music Chart (Rudiments of Music)	2
Foreword and Explanation	3
Diagram for C Position	4
Right Hand—Left Hand (Alone)	5
Two Hands (Part 1 and 2)	5
Skipping Notes (Part 1 and 2)	6
R.H. and L.H. in Quarter Notes	7
Left Hand Song	8
Right Hand Song	9
Chords in Left Hand	10
Whole Note March	11
Easy Waltz	12
Half Note March	13
Snappy Polka	13
Robin Hood	14
Gliding Along	15
R.H. High C Position	16
L.H. 5th Finger Extended to B	16
Sunset Waltz	17
Silverbell Polka	17
Diagram for G Position	18
Songs in G Position	19
Vacation Waltz	20
L.H. 5th Finger Extends to F♯	20
Moonlight	21
Sunrise Polka	21
Lightly Row	22
R.H. Study in Thirds	23
The Cuckoo	23
My Little Pinto Pal	24
R.H. Chord Building	25
Evening Breezes	25
Note Spelling Page	26
High C Position in Thirds	27
It's June Again	27
The Big Parade	28
F Position Diagram	30
Songs in F Position	31
Sunny Skies	32
L.H. 5th Finger Extended to E	32
Sweet Dreams	33
Fun With Broken Chords	34
Lazy Mary	35
America	36

Cover and Song Illustrations by Harry M. Carlisle

Course consists of: Preparatory Book; Book One; Book Two and Book Three.

Printed in U. S. A.

MUSIC CHART

Rudiments of Music

The number beside the note, indicates the line or space of each note.

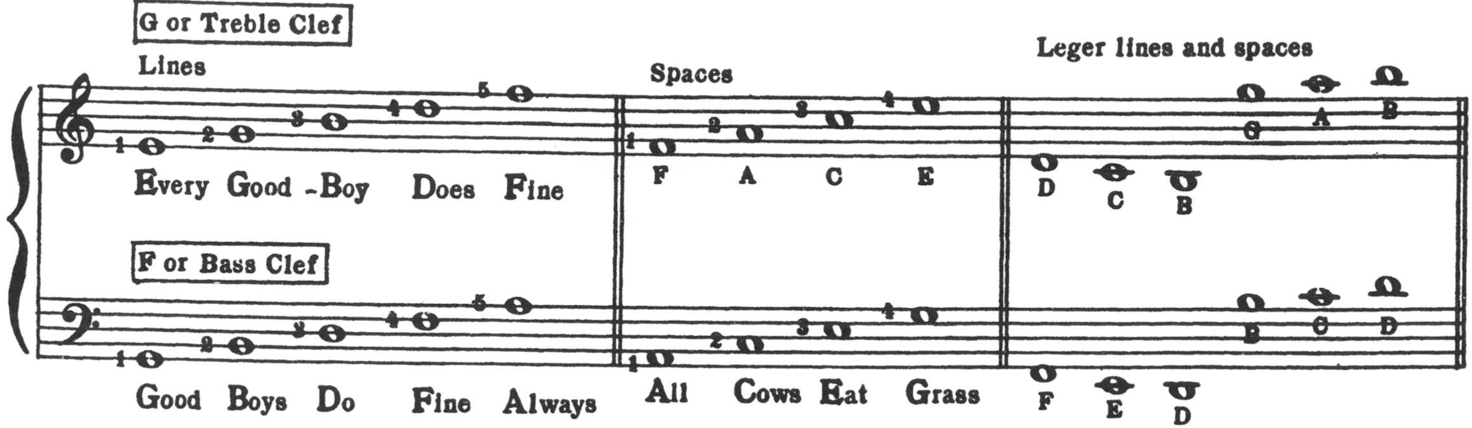
G or Treble Clef
Lines
1 2 3 4 5
Every Good -Boy Does Fine
Spaces
1 2 3 4
F A C E
Leger lines and spaces
D C B
G A B
F or Bass Clef
1 2 3 4 5
Good Boys Do Fine Always
1 2 3 4
All Cows Eat Grass
F E D
B C D

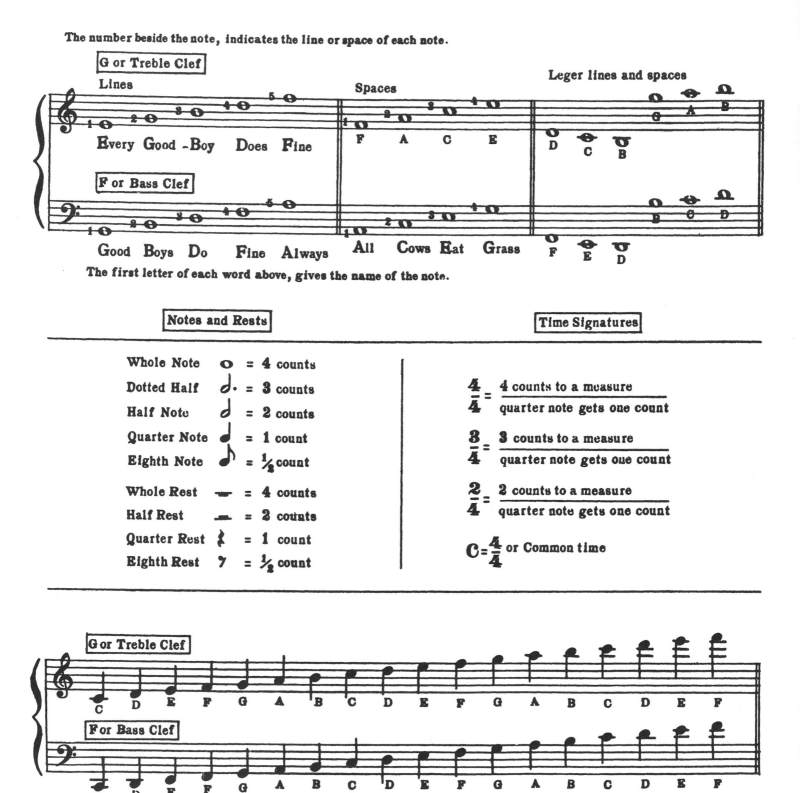

The first letter of each word above, gives the name of the note.

Notes and Rests

Whole Note	𝅝	= 4 counts
Dotted Half	𝅗𝅥.	= 3 counts
Half Note	𝅗𝅥	= 2 counts
Quarter Note	♩	= 1 count
Eighth Note	♪	= ½ count
Whole Rest	𝄻	= 4 counts
Half Rest	𝄼	= 2 counts
Quarter Rest	𝄽	= 1 count
Eighth Rest	𝄾	= ½ count

Time Signatures

$\frac{4}{4} = \frac{\text{4 counts to a measure}}{\text{quarter note gets one count}}$

$\frac{3}{4} = \frac{\text{3 counts to a measure}}{\text{quarter note gets one count}}$

$\frac{2}{4} = \frac{\text{2 counts to a measure}}{\text{quarter note gets one count}}$

C = $\frac{4}{4}$ or Common time

G or Treble Clef
C D E F G A B C D E F G A B C D E F
F or Bass Clef
C D E F G A B C D E F G A B C D E F

Refer to this page as you would a dictionary.

Foreword

The Aims and Principles of the Everybody Likes the Piano Course

— Book One —

The Aim of the Course is to teach and train the piano student beginner so that he has a sound foundation for either classical or popular music, or both; to develop correct fingering and finger control; to teach note reading; to develop the sense of rhythm through rhythmic arrangements; to begin the study of harmony and chord construction. This course is suitable for either private or class instruction.

The following principles are the most successful in achieving these primary aims.

1) The use and development of the Five Finger position in the keys of C.G. and F. with occasional finger extensions. This teaches the student to read notes, and learn their names. It insures correct fingering by keeping the hands in position, also strengthens all fingers equally.

2) The use of easy bass patterns in a steady rhythmic style. The harmonious arrangements develope a strong left hand, necessary to a good pianist. A knowledge of chords and their construction is essential, and it is best to have this knowledge from the very first. This is important for sight reading and analysis.

3) Gradual, logical step by step approach, which builds a strong foundation, and insures progress. This allows the student who grasps the material readily to proceed rapidly, with a secure background of concrete knowledge. A pupil with slower comprehension will find the very gradualness of the course enables him to learn without excessive effort.

4) The use of simple tunes and familiar melodies. These increase the student's interest, and are an incentive to better playing.

The success of all endeavors is built on a good foundation. Do not skip pages, as each page is your stepping stone to the next page. For your own advantage, do not omit any reading matter. Practice faithfully, and carefully, and follow instructions. Have faith in yourself, be sincere, and be patient. Most important, use common sense, and imagination. Remember that Music is an Art.

Joseph M. Estella

C Position

1. BLACK KEYS are in groups of TWO and THREE.
2. C is the first white key to the left of group of two blacks.
3. At the beginning we will develop the student's hands to play in the C Position.
4. We will learn the notes and piano keys by their names; C.D.E.F.G. etc.
5. The numbers indicate the fingers that must be used and followed in playing.

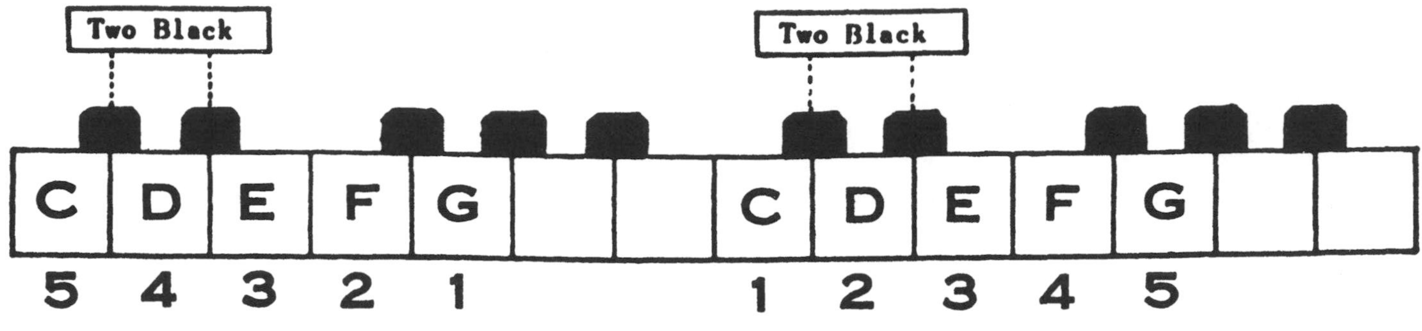
Two Black
Two Black
C D E F G
C D E F G
5 4 3 2 1
1 2 3 4 5

To obtain the correct position of the hands it is best that all the fingers are pressed down together.

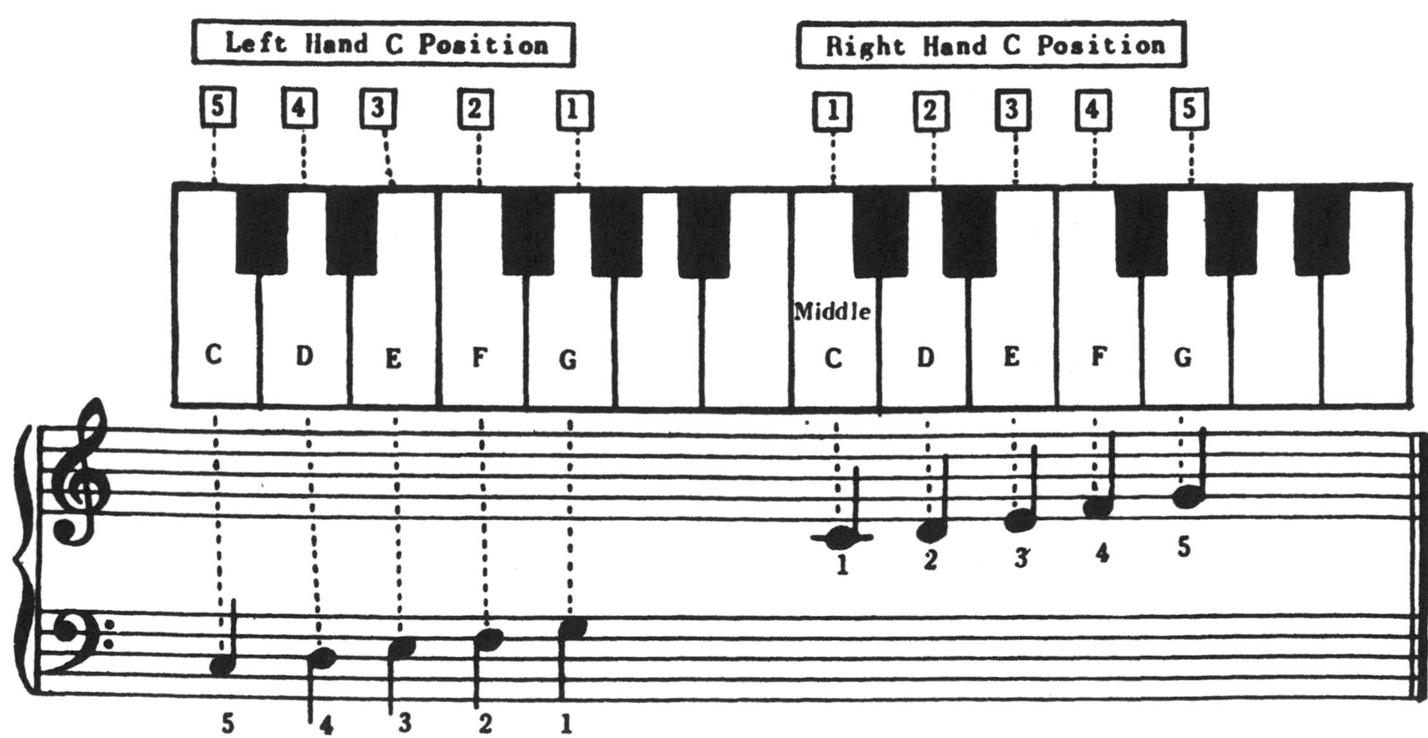
Left Hand C Position
Right Hand C Position
5 4 3 2 1
1 2 3 4 5
C D E F G
Middle C D E F G
1 2 3 4 5
5 4 3 2 1

Placing the Fingers over the Keys

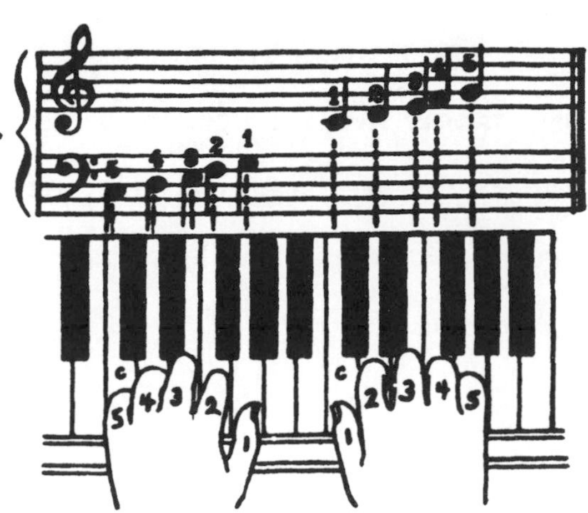

- The Piano has only twelve different keys or notes. (Seven white and five black)
- Music uses only the first seven letters of the alphabet(A-B-C-D-E-F-G)

Right Hand

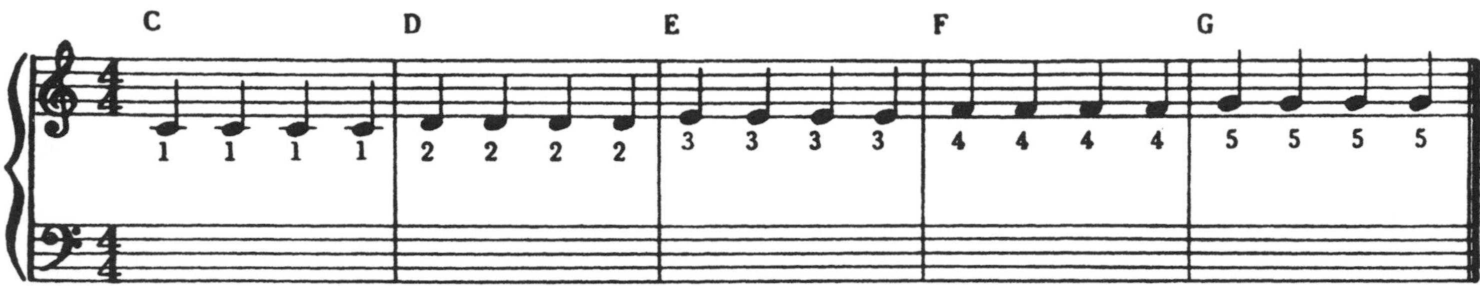
C
D
E
F
G
1 1 1 1
2 2 2 2
3 3 3 3
4 4 4 4
5 5 5 5

In playing these first two songs (Right Hand and Left Hand), hold all fingers down and play only each finger alone as you come to it. This will help strengthen each individual finger.

Left Hand

C
D
E
F
G
5 5 5 5
4 4 4 4
3 3 3 3
2 2 2 2
1 1 1 1

Two Hands (part I)

1
2
3
4
5
5
4
3
2
1

Do not hold all fingers down now, but lift them up and hold close above the keys.

(Be sure to keep hands in perfect C position)

Two Hands (part II)

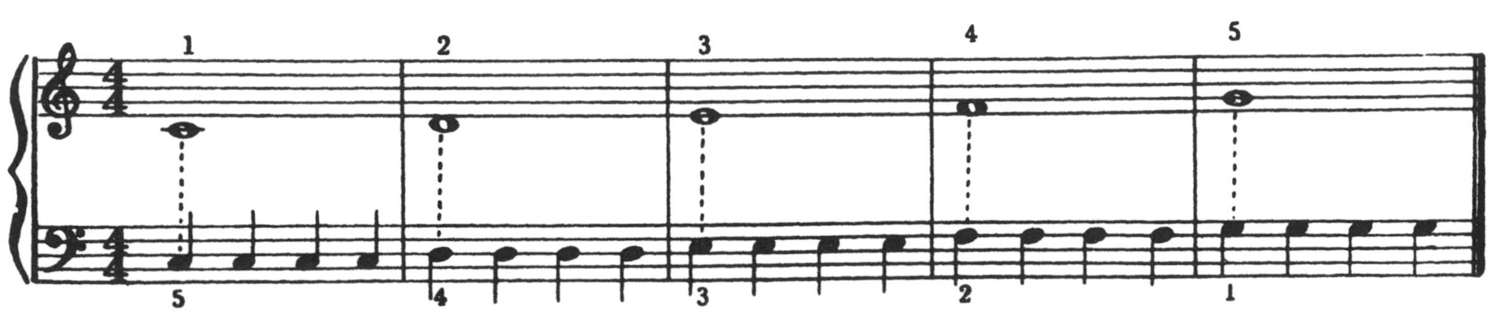
1
2
3
4
5
5
4
3
2
1

Skipping Notes (I)

A QUARTER NOTE (♩) gets ONE (1) count.

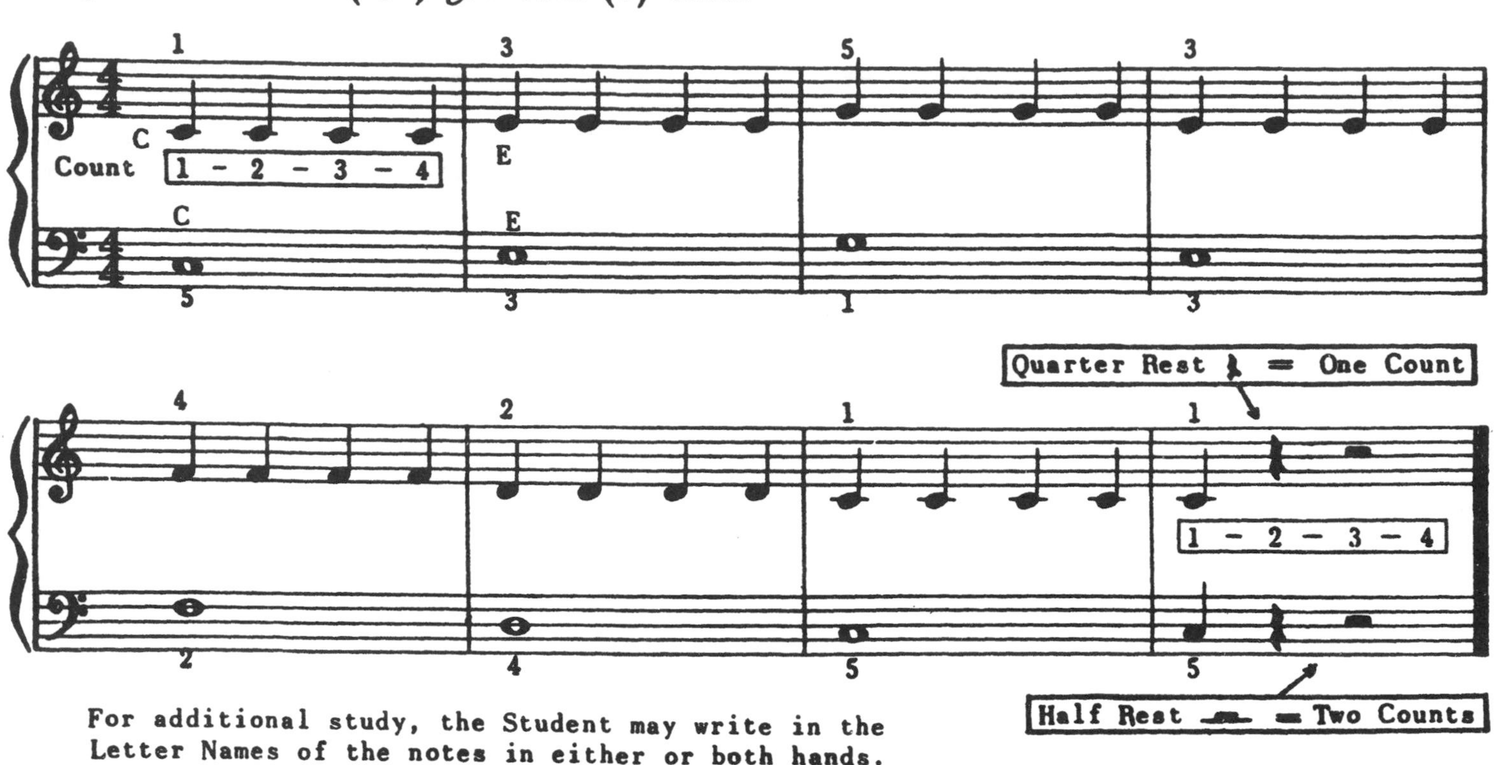
C
Count
1 - 2 - 3 - 4
E
C
E
Quarter Rest = One Count
1 - 2 - 3 - 4
Half Rest = Two Counts

For additional study, the Student may write in the Letter Names of the notes in either or both hands. (*Refer to pages 2 or 4*)

Skipping Notes (II)

A WHOLE NOTE (o) gets FOUR (4) counts.

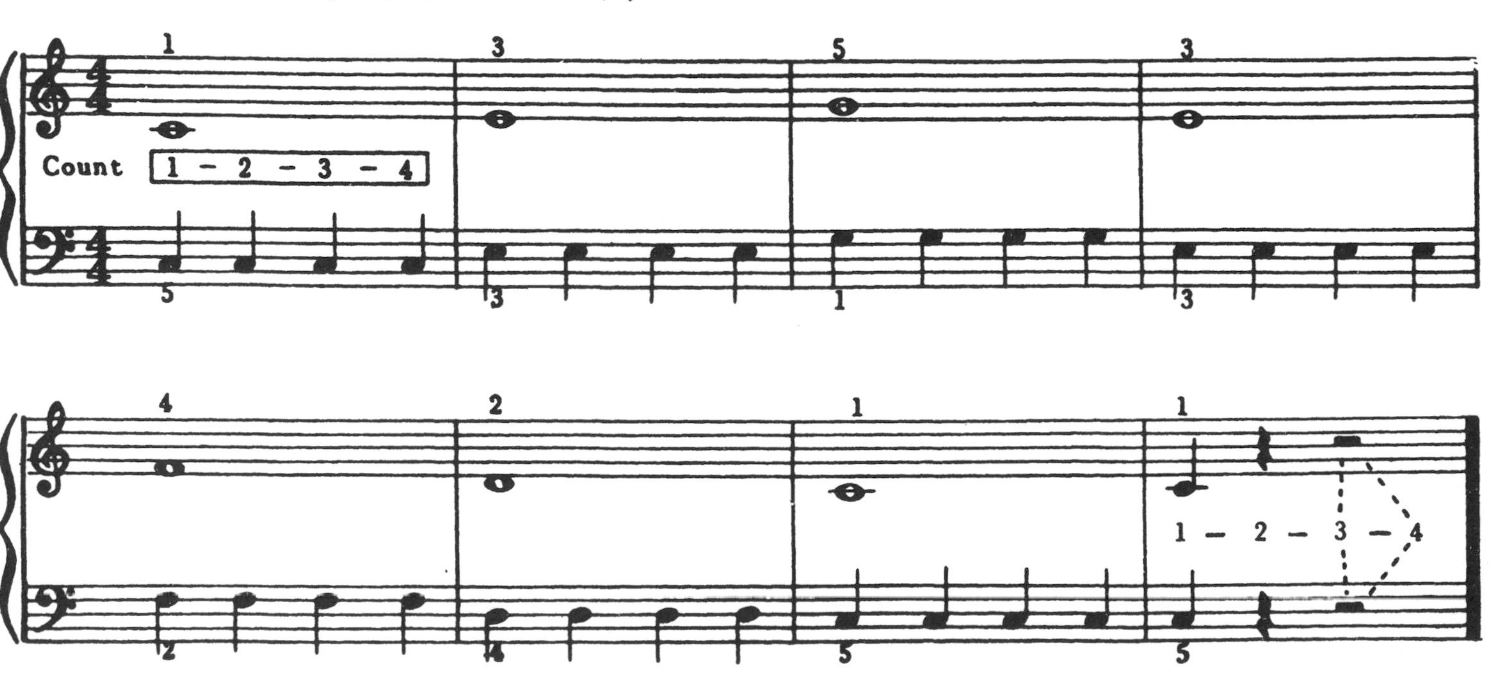
Count
1 - 2 - 3 - 4
1 - 2 - 3 - 4

Right Hand in Quarter Notes

1
3
2
4
Count
1 – 2 – 3
5
3
4
2
3
5
1
1
3
1
5
5

A DOTTED HALF NOTE (𝅗𝅥.) gets THREE (3) counts.

Left Hand in Quarter Notes

1
3
2
4
5
3
4
2
3
5
1
1
3
1
5
5

Left Hand Song

Student may write in the Letter-Names of the notes below.

Count
1 — 2 — 3
C E G
5 3 1
1 3 5

Play the three notes together lightly.

(Lift the L.H. up by bending at the wrist and coming down lightly)

D F G
4 2 1
1 2 4

5 3 1
1 3 5

4 2 1
1 2 4
5 3 1
1 3 5

Right Hand Song

Student may write in the Letter-Names of the Right Hand notes.

1
3
5
5
C
E
G
Count
1 — 2 — 3
1
3
5

2
4
5
5
D
F
G
1
2
4

1
3
5
5
1
3
5

2
4
5
5
1
3
5
5
3
1
1
2
4
1
3
5

Left Hand Chords

A chord= *Two or more sounds or tones heard at the same time. They may be played;*

(1) As a solid chord all notes together.

(2) As broken chords one or two notes at a time.

C chord
Tonic chord is built on the 1st note of scale.
Solid chord
Broken chords
G
E
C
C
G
E
G7 chord
Dominant 7th is built on the 5th note of scale.
G
F
D
D
G
F
C = Tonic or (I) chord in Key of C
Note The G7 chord contains the notes(G-B-D-F),however it is possible to use different combinations of these and still keep the G7 chord harmony.
G7 = Dom. 7th or (V7) chord in Key of C
C
Left Hand in 4/4 Time
C
G7
C

Chords should be learned by knowing the names of the notes which make up the chord.

Example C *chord is* (C-E-G)

(MARCHING SOLDIERS)

Whole Note March

Bring out Right Hand melody.

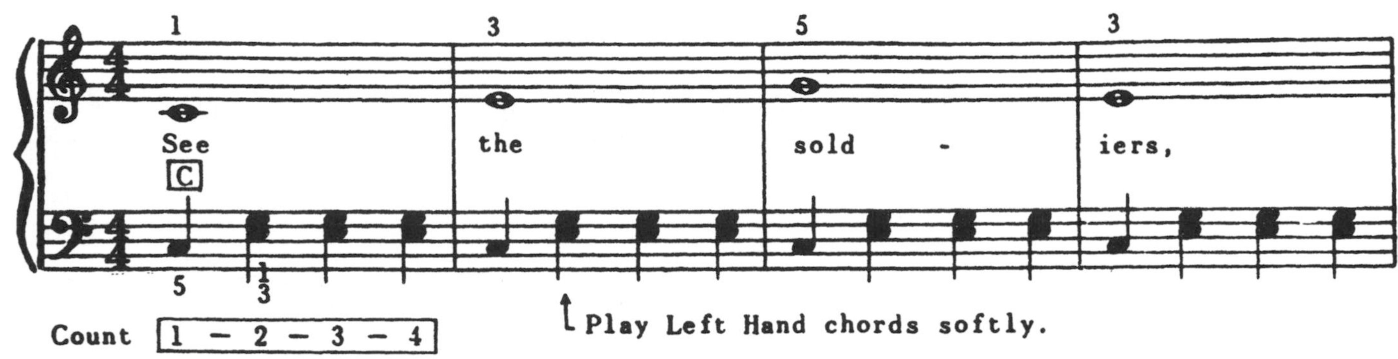
1
3
5
3
See
the
sold -
iers,
C
5
1
3
Count 1 - 2 - 3 - 4
Play Left Hand chords softly.

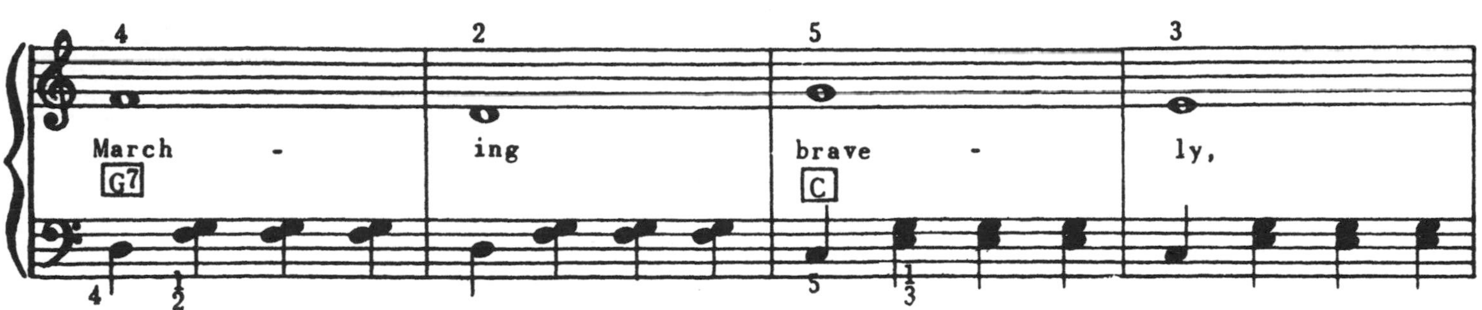
4
2
5
3
March -
ing
brave -
ly,
G7
C
4
1
2
5
1
3

1
3
5
3
See
the
sold -
iers,
5
1
3

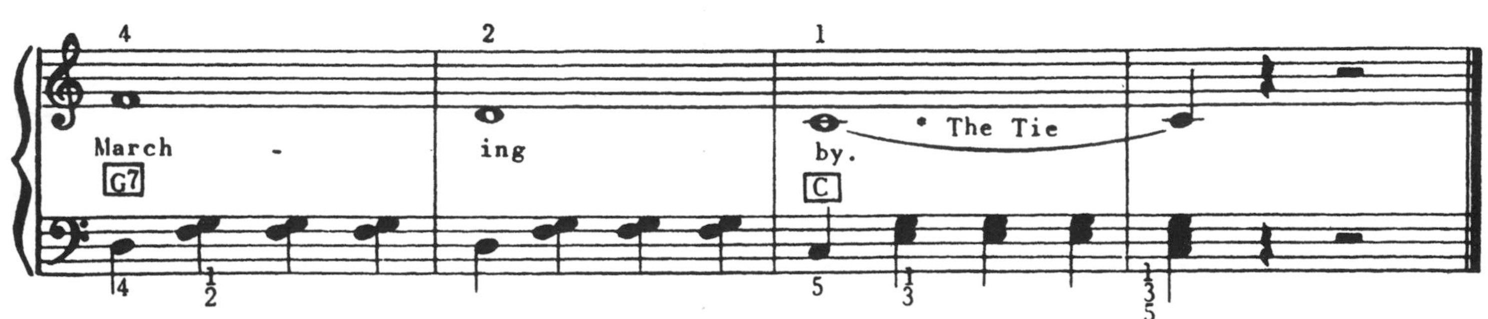
4
2
1
March -
ing
by.
* The Tie
G7
C
4
1
2
5
1
3
1
3
5

* The Tie is a curved line placed between two notes of the pitch. You play only the first note and hold down for the total value of both notes.

Easy Waltz

Moderato = (Moderate tempo)
I like waltz - ing,
waltz - ing, waltz - ing;
I like waltz - ing,
Dear with you.
Count 1 - 2 - 3
Left Hand in 2/4 Time
Count 1 — 2

* Write in chord names as they occur in the Easy Waltz.

Half Note March

f = Loud

Two dots:
Repeat signs

A HALF NOTE (𝅗𝅥) gets TWO (2) counts.

Snappy Polka

mf = Medium loud

Robin Hood

Moderato

mf

(Remember to play L.H. chords lightly)

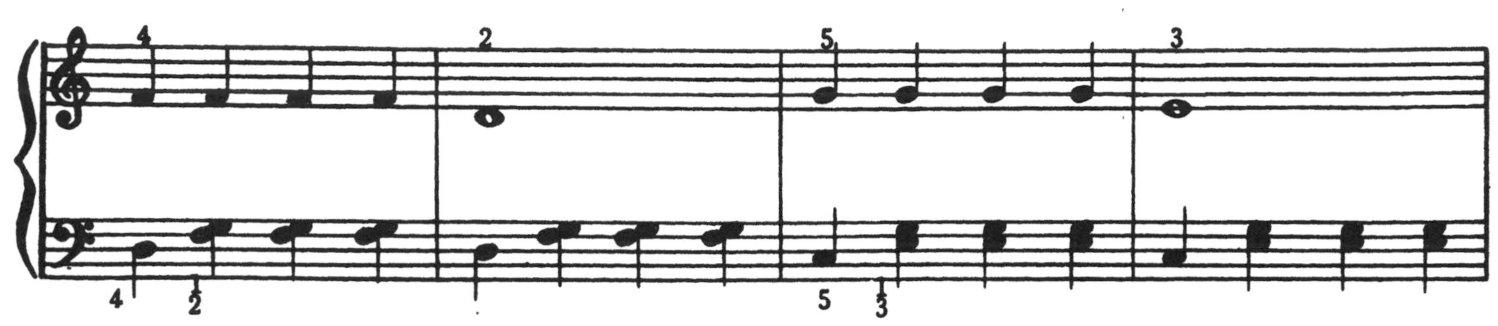

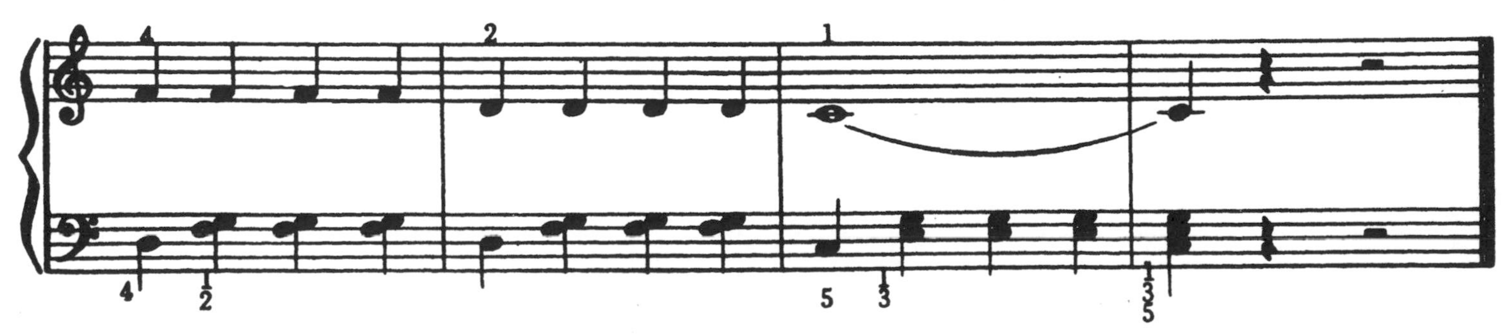

On the following page, you will notice curved lines over groups of notes. These lines are called slurs, and divide the music into phrases, which are played in a smooth connected manner.

Gliding Along

+)(Arpeggio Waltz)

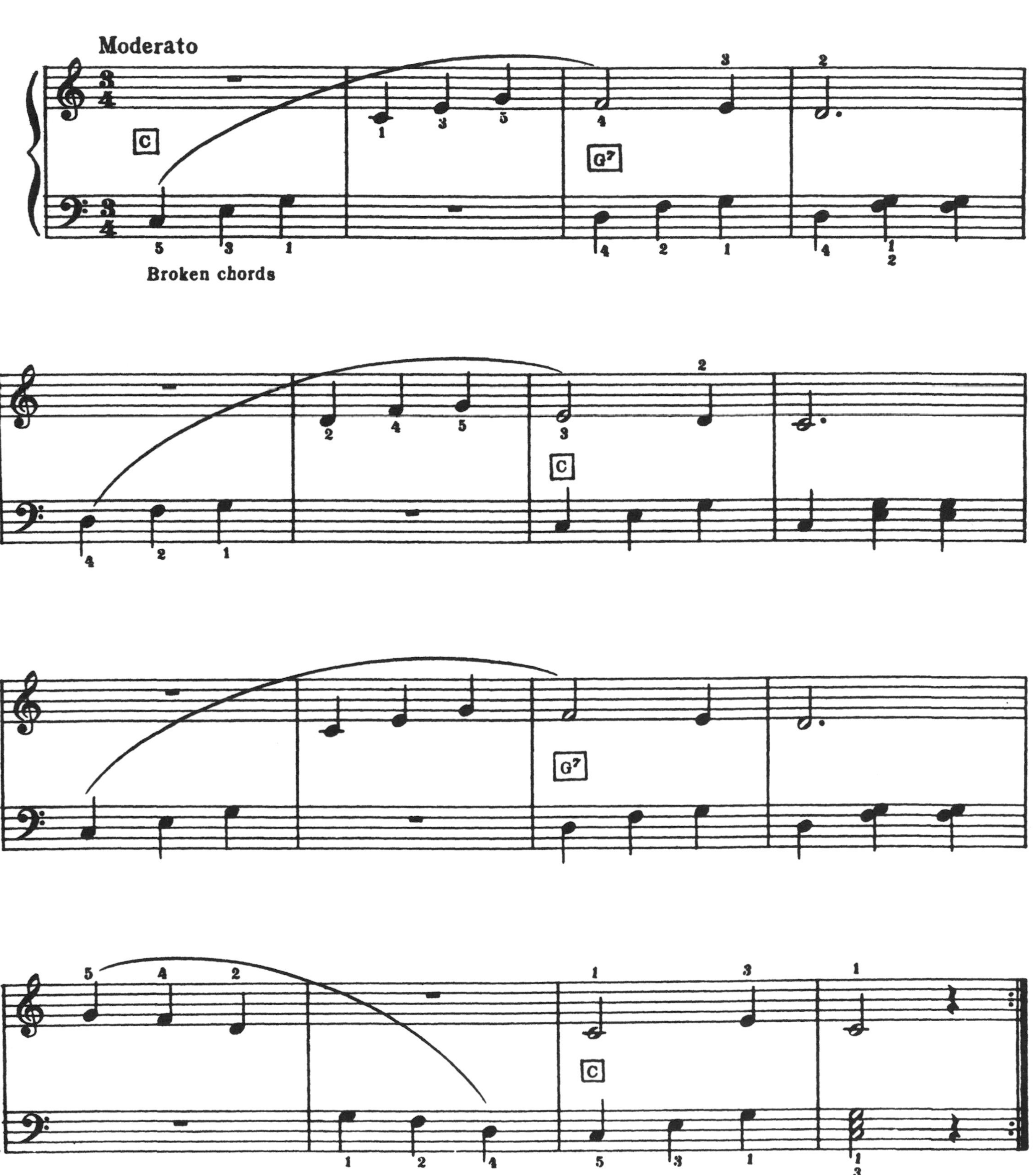
Moderato
C
G7
C
G7
C
Broken chords

+) An Arpeggio is a broken chord.

Right Hand Mid. C Position

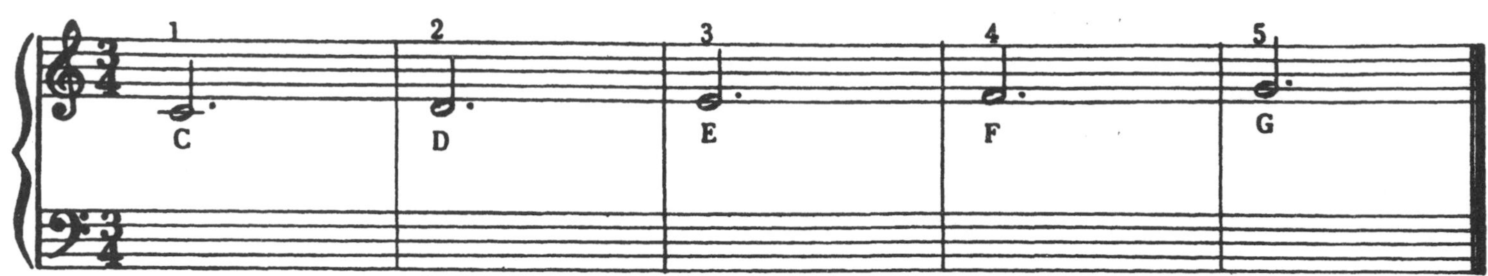
1
2
3
4
5
C
D
E
F
G

Right Hand High C Position

(Next position above Middle C position)

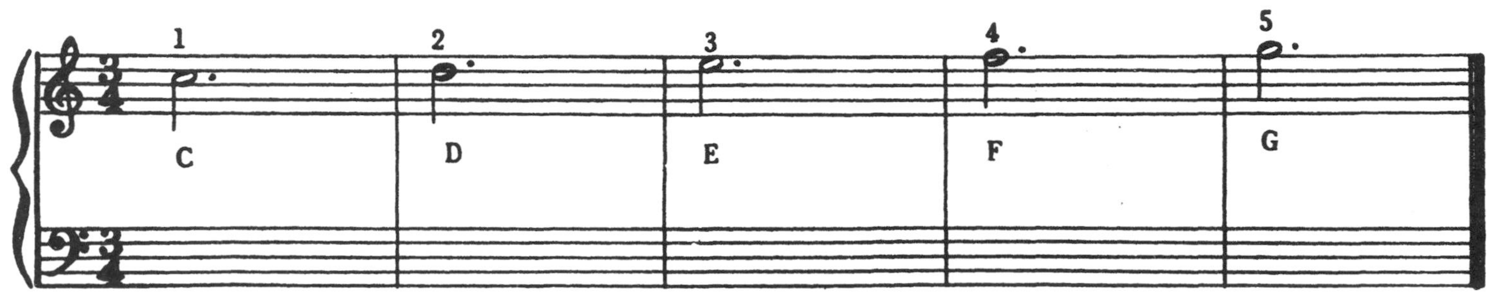
1
2
3
4
5
C
D
E
F
G

Left Hand 5th Finger Extended to B

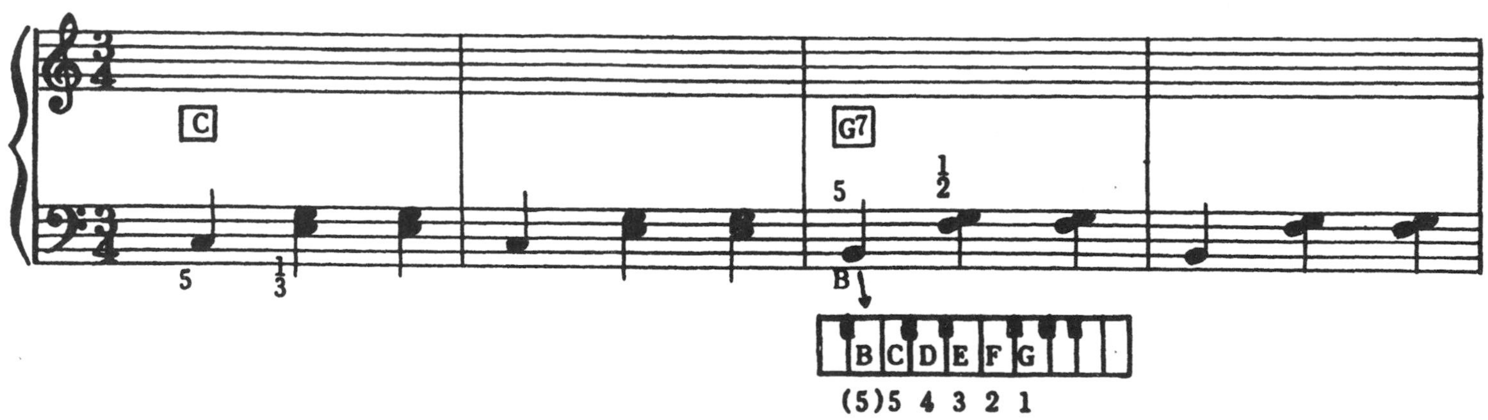
C
G7
5
1/3
5
1/2
B
B C D E F G
(5)5 4 3 2 1

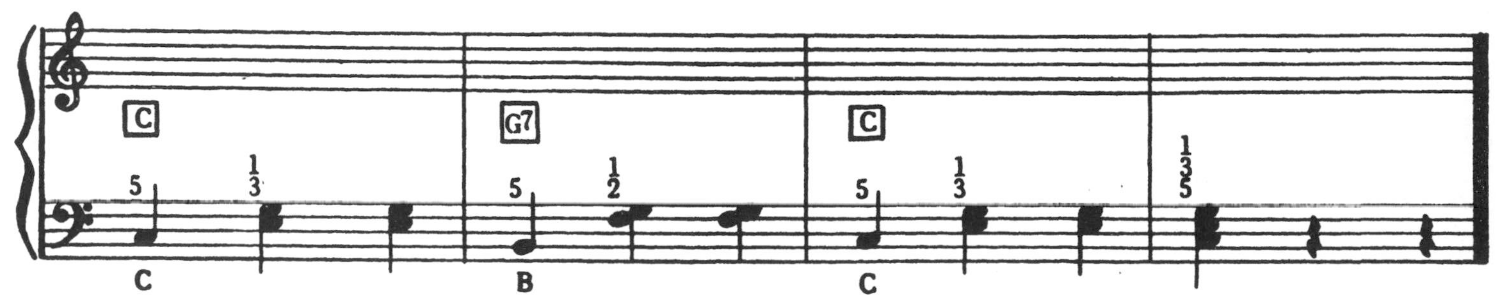
C
G7
C
5
1/3
5
1/2
5
1/3
1/3/5
C
B
C

Sunset Waltz

mp = Medium soft

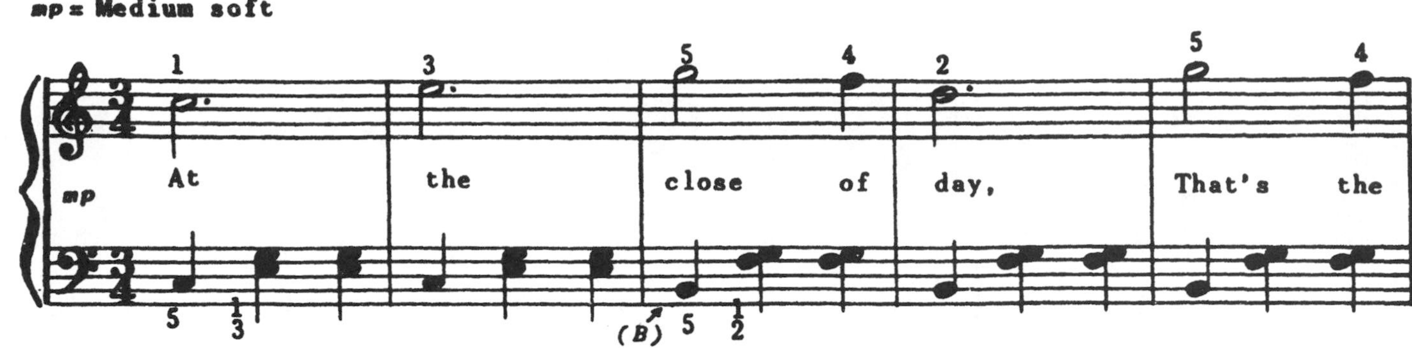
mp
At the close of day, That's the
(B)

time when we say; "Look o'er yon - der

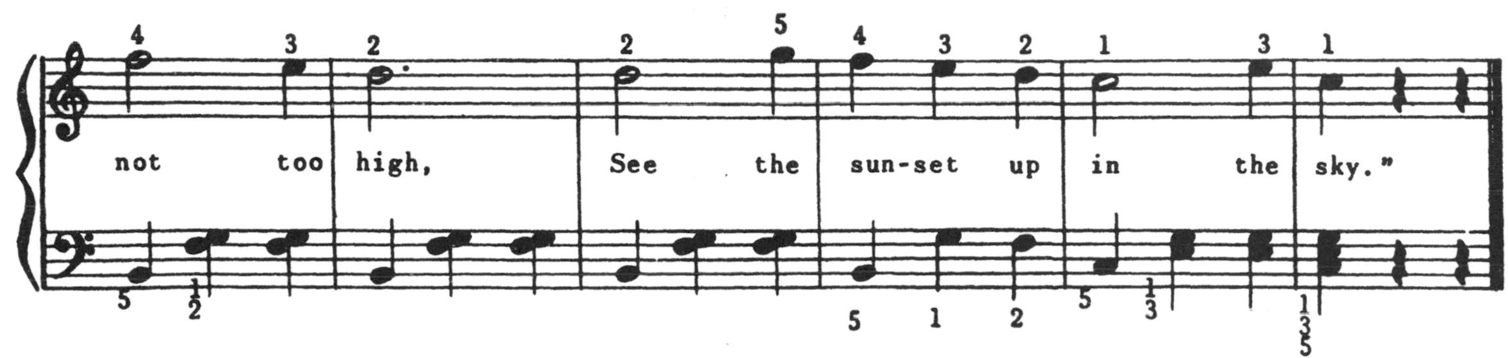
not too high, See the sun-set up in the sky."

Silverbell Polka

* Allegro

mf

* Allegro = *Quick or lively.*

G Hand Position

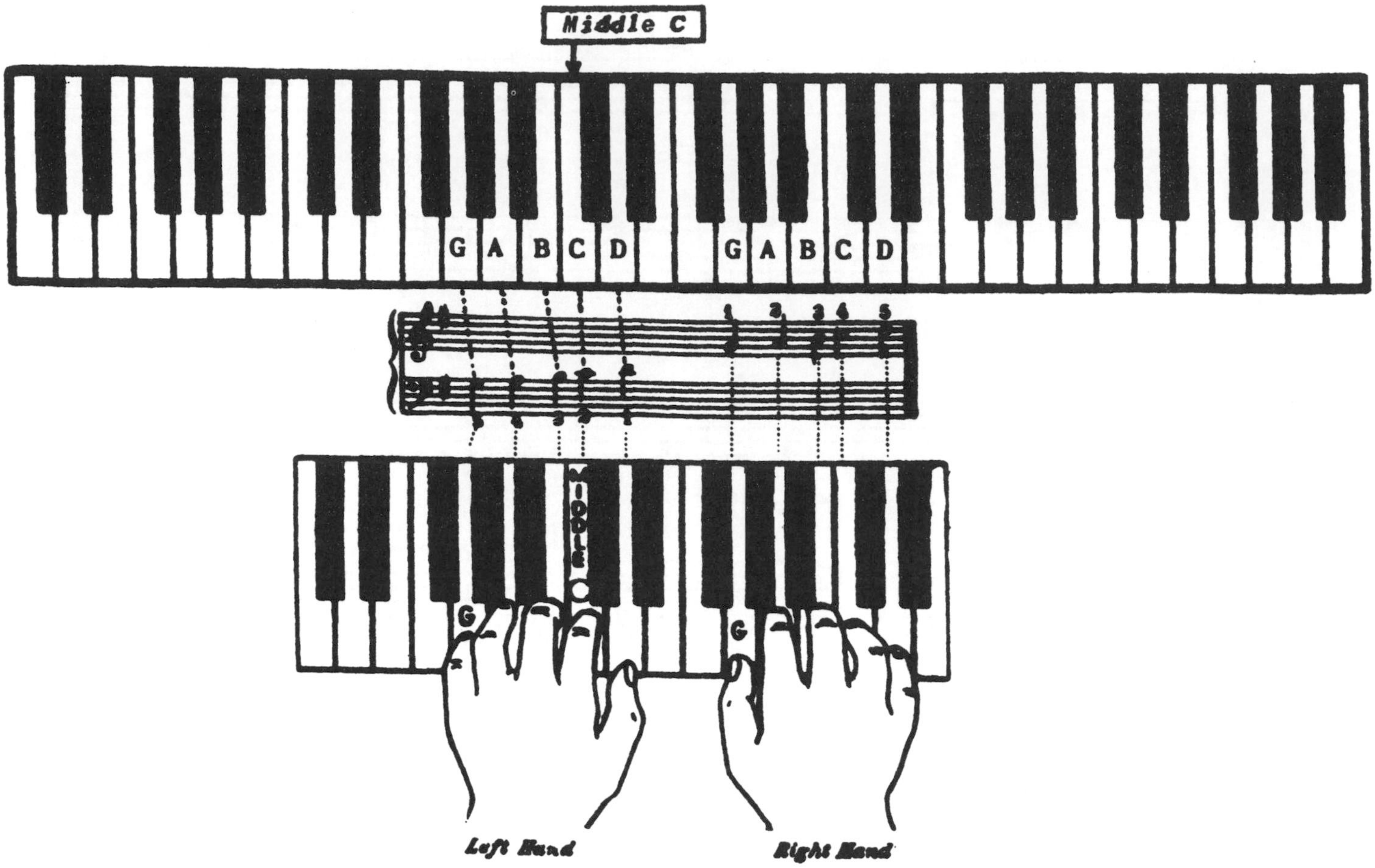

Middle C

G A B C D G A B C D

MIDDLE C

Left Hand Right Hand

Quarter Notes in Right Hand

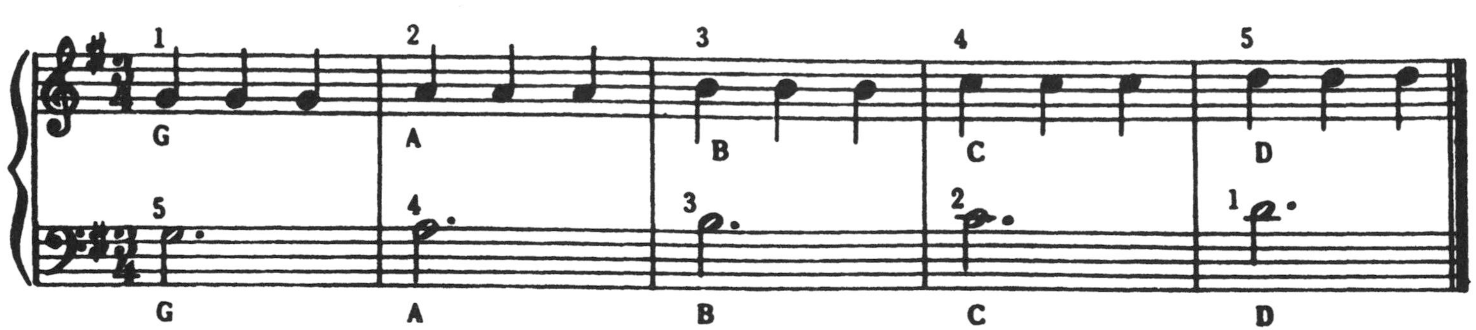
1 2 3 4 5
G A B C D
5 4 3 2 1
G A B C D

Quarter Notes in Left Hand

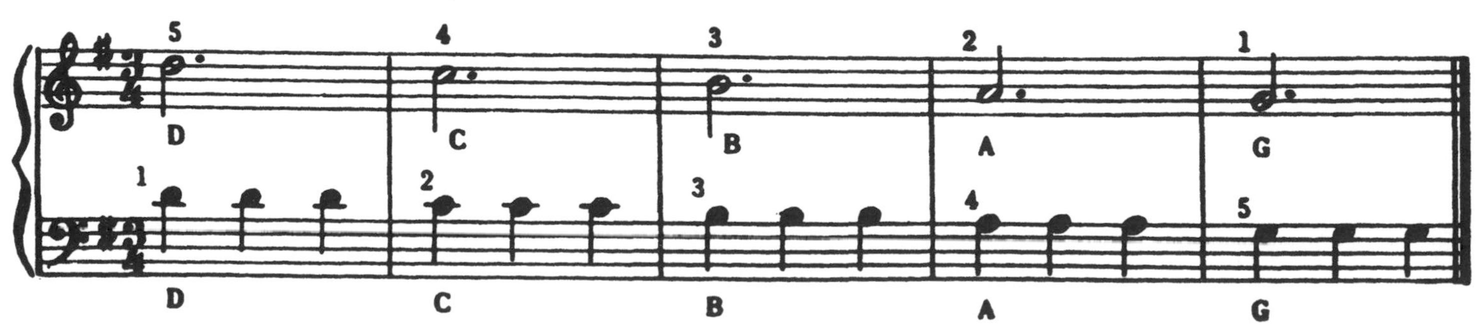
5 4 3 2 1
D C B A G
1 2 3 4 5
D C B A G

Left Hand Song in G Position

Key of G *(Every F#)*

G
B
D
5
3
1
G
Chord
D
B
G
1
3
5
A
C
D
4
2
1
D7
Chord
D
C
A
1
2
4
5
3
1
G
1
3
5

(In the Key of G) G chord is the Tonic (I) and D7 is the Dom.7th (V7)

Right Hand Song in G Position

Student may write in the Letter-Names in the song below. *(Refer to page 18)*

1
3
5
5
G
1
3
5
2
4
5
5
1
3
5
5
3
1
D7
1
2
4
G
1
3
5

Vacation Waltz

Moderato
Now, hap - py days,
G
Are com - ing near;
D7
G
Va - ca - tion soon
will be here.
D7
G
Left Hand 5th Finger Extended to F♯
G
D7
G
F♯ G A B C D
(5) 5 4 3 2 1

Moonlight

Andantino

mp
Moon - light night, Stars

Write in chord names in this song. *(Remember to sharp every F in the L.H.)*

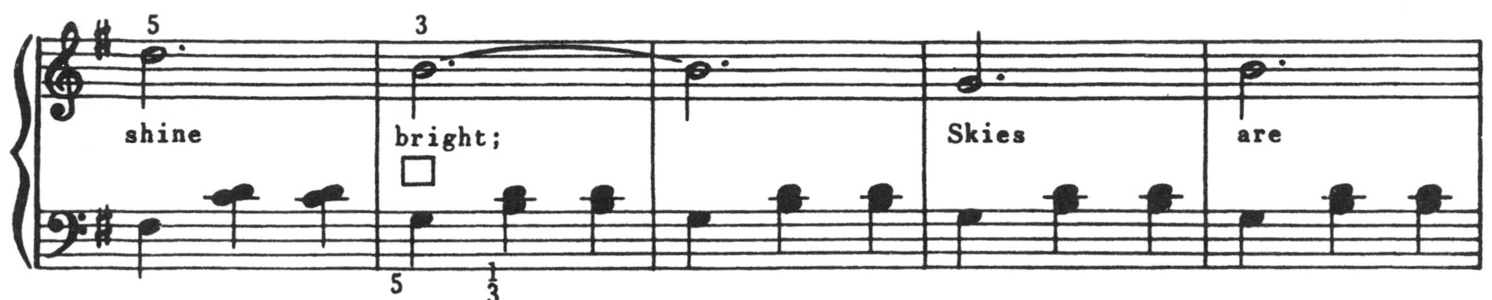
shine bright; Skies are

clear, Wish you were here.

Andantino = *(Somewhat slower)*

Sunrise Polka

* Allegretto

mf

* *Gay and rather lively.*

Lightly Row
* G
D7
G
mp
Light-ly Row ! Light-ly Row! o'er the glass-y waves we go;
G
D7
G
Smooth-ly glide ! smooth-ly glide! on the si - lent tide.
D7
G
Let the winds and wa - ters be, ming-led with our mel - o - dy;
G
D7
G
Sing and float! sing and float! in our lit-tle boat.

* The chord names or symbols may be used for the guitar, uke, etc.

Right Hand Study in Thirds

G position

The Cuckoo

Dolce = *Sweetly*

G — D⁷ — G

Cuck - oo, Cuck - oo, wel - come thy song,

D⁷ — G

Cuck - oo, Cuck - oo, sing all day long,

D⁷ — G

Win - ter is go - ing, soft breez - es blow - ing,

D⁷ — G

Spring - time, spring - time soon will be here.

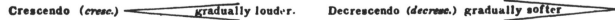

Crescendo (*cresc.*) gradually louder. Decrescendo (*decresc.*) gradually softer

E.S.& Co.5309

Middle C Position in Thirds

My Little Pinto Pal

Allegretto
C
G7
C
mf
G7
C

Note: When dots are written above or below notes you play with a staccato touch. (See next page.)

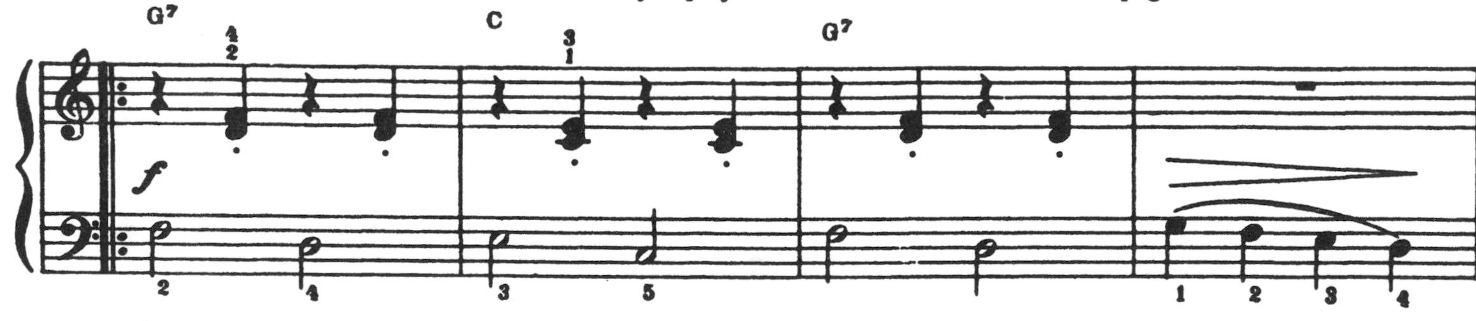
G7
C
G7
f

(Bring out L.H. Melody)

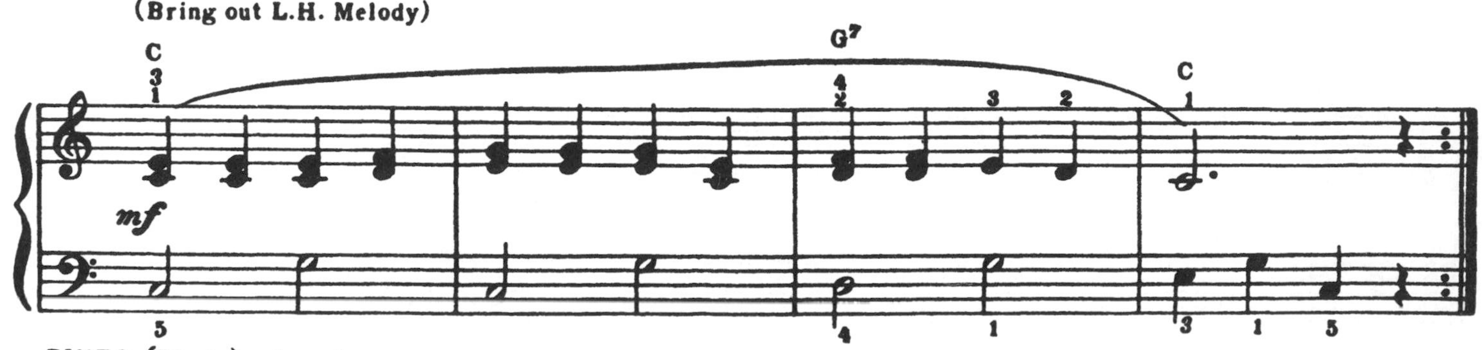
C
G7
C
mf

PINTO (Pin-to) : A western cow-pony

Return to the Repeat Signs
(Beginning of third line)

Right Hand Chord Building

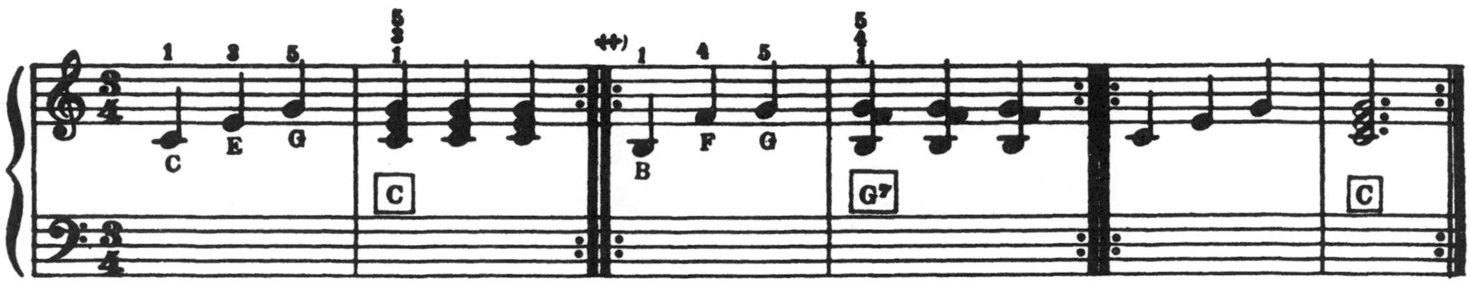
1 3 5
5 3 1
++) 1 4 5
5 4 1
C E G
B F G
C
G7
C

++) 1st finger extended down to B.

Evening Breezes

(Play R.H. chords lightly, with a +) staccato touch.)

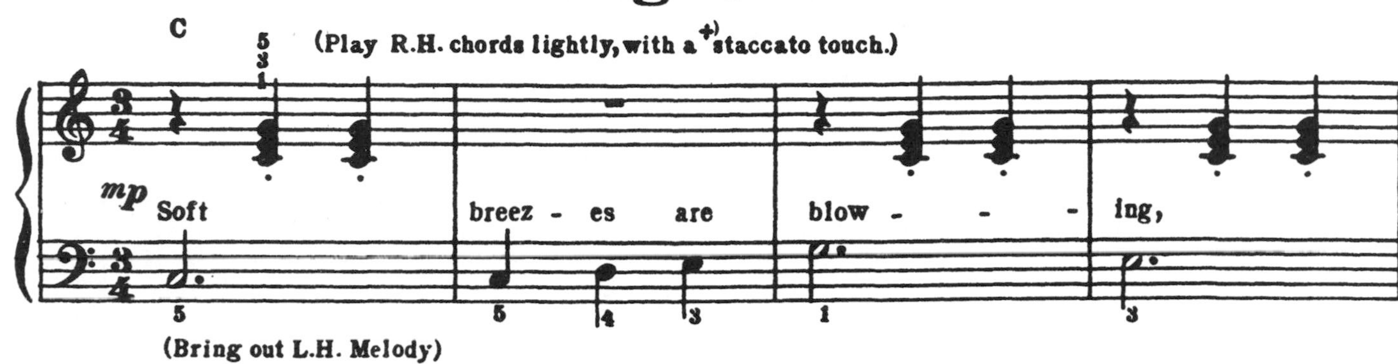
C
5 3 1
mp
Soft breez - es are blow - - - ing,
5 5 4 3 1 3
(Bring out L.H. Melody)

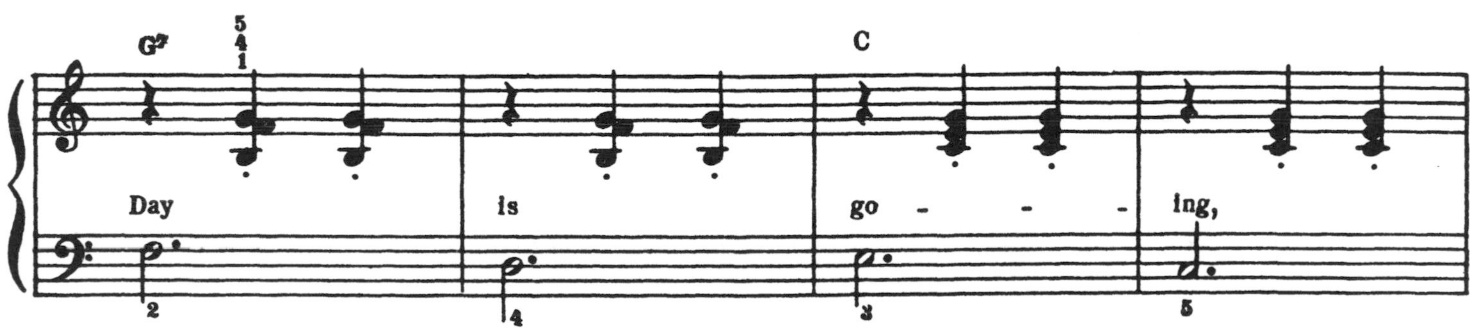
G7
5 4 1
C
Day is go - - - ing,
2 4 3 5

Shad - - - ows of the eve - - - ning,

G7
C
Gent - - - ly fall.
5

+) Staccato = In a crisp, separated or detached style.

Note Spelling Page

(Name all Notes on this page)

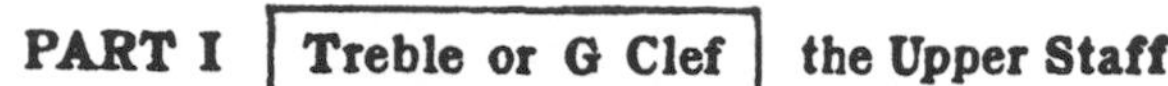
PART I
Treble or G Clef
the Upper Staff

Lines
1 2 3 4 5
(Write in Names below)
E G B D F
(G)

Spaces
1 2 3 4
F A C E
(A)

Find the Words Below
(Lines and Spaces combined)

PART II
Bass or F Clef
the Lower Staff

Lines
Write in Names below
G B D F A
(B)
1 2 3 4 5

Spaces
A C E G
(F)
1 2 3 4

Find the Words Below
(Lines and Spaces combined)

High C Position in Thirds

High C position

(WALTZ IN THIRDS)

It's June Again

Moderato

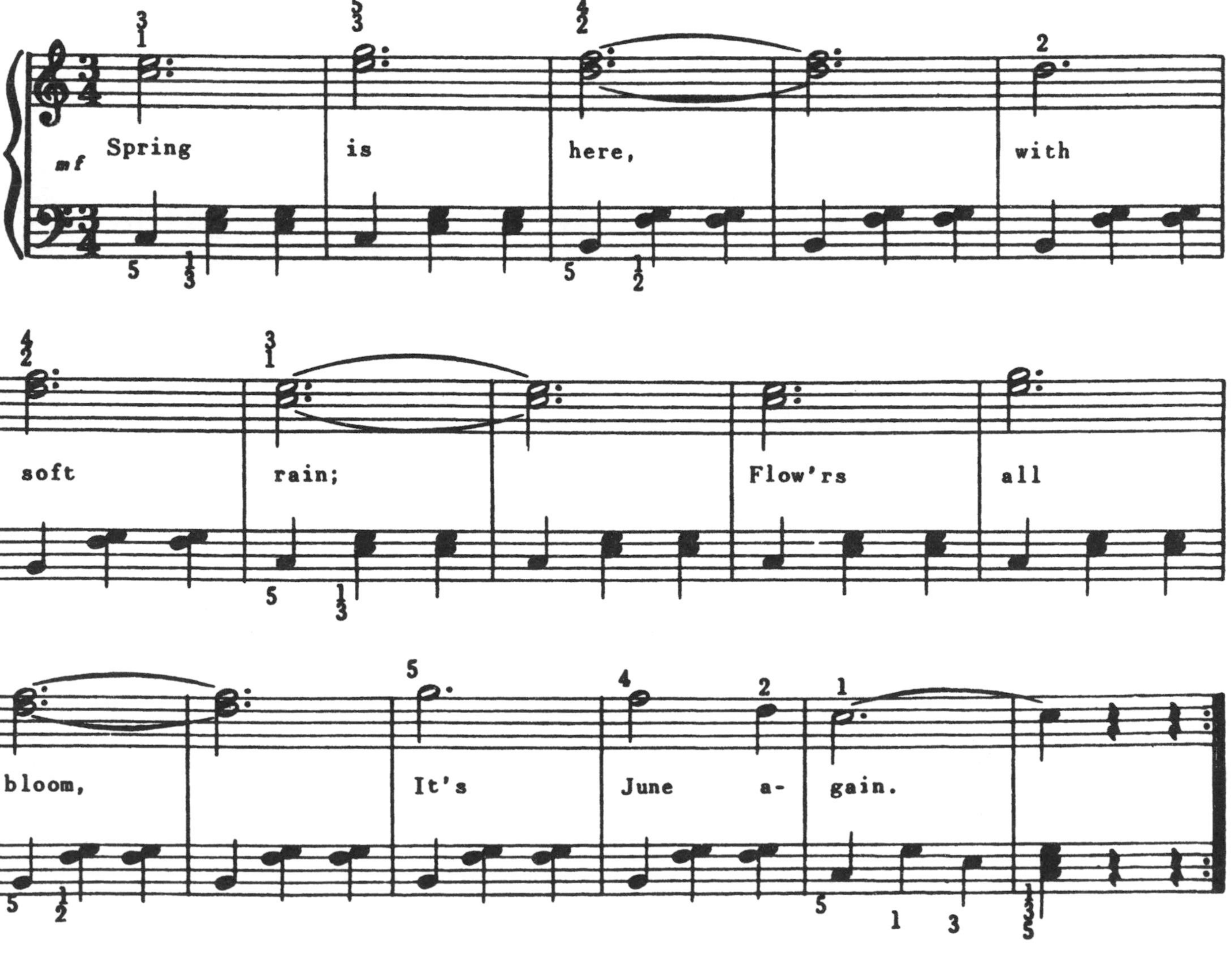

mf

Spring is here, with soft rain; Flow'rs all bloom, It's June a- gain.

The Big Parade

* Marcato

*(Play distinctly and with an accent)

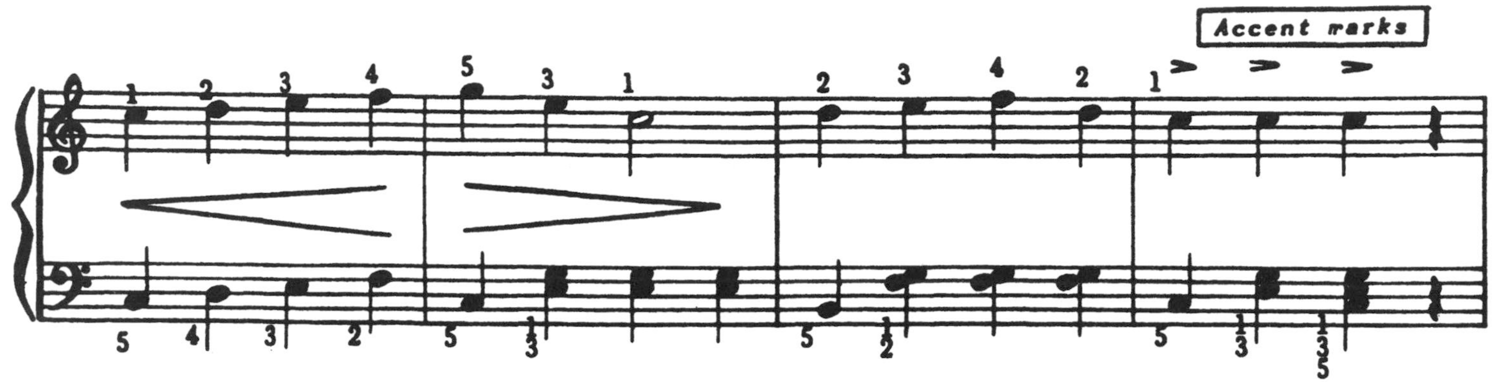
Accent marks

E.S.& Co. 5309

The Big Parade makes an excellent RECITAL PIECE

(Shift to G position)

mf

(Repeat G Position)

(Shift back to High C position)

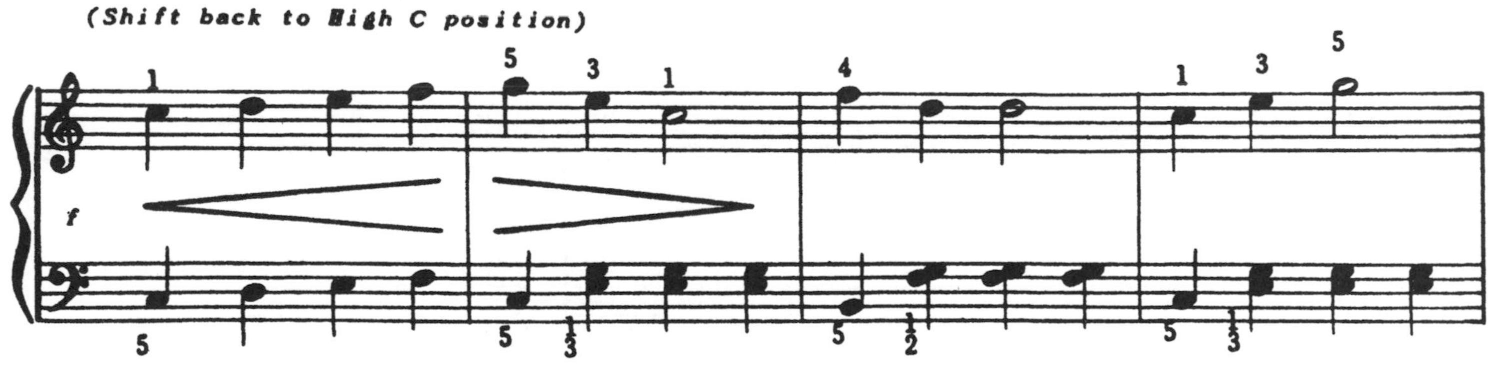
f

Supplemental Piece "FIREFLY POLKA" by Joseph Estella

— A fine entertaining piece that may be used at this point. —

F Hand Position

Key of F *(Every Bb)*

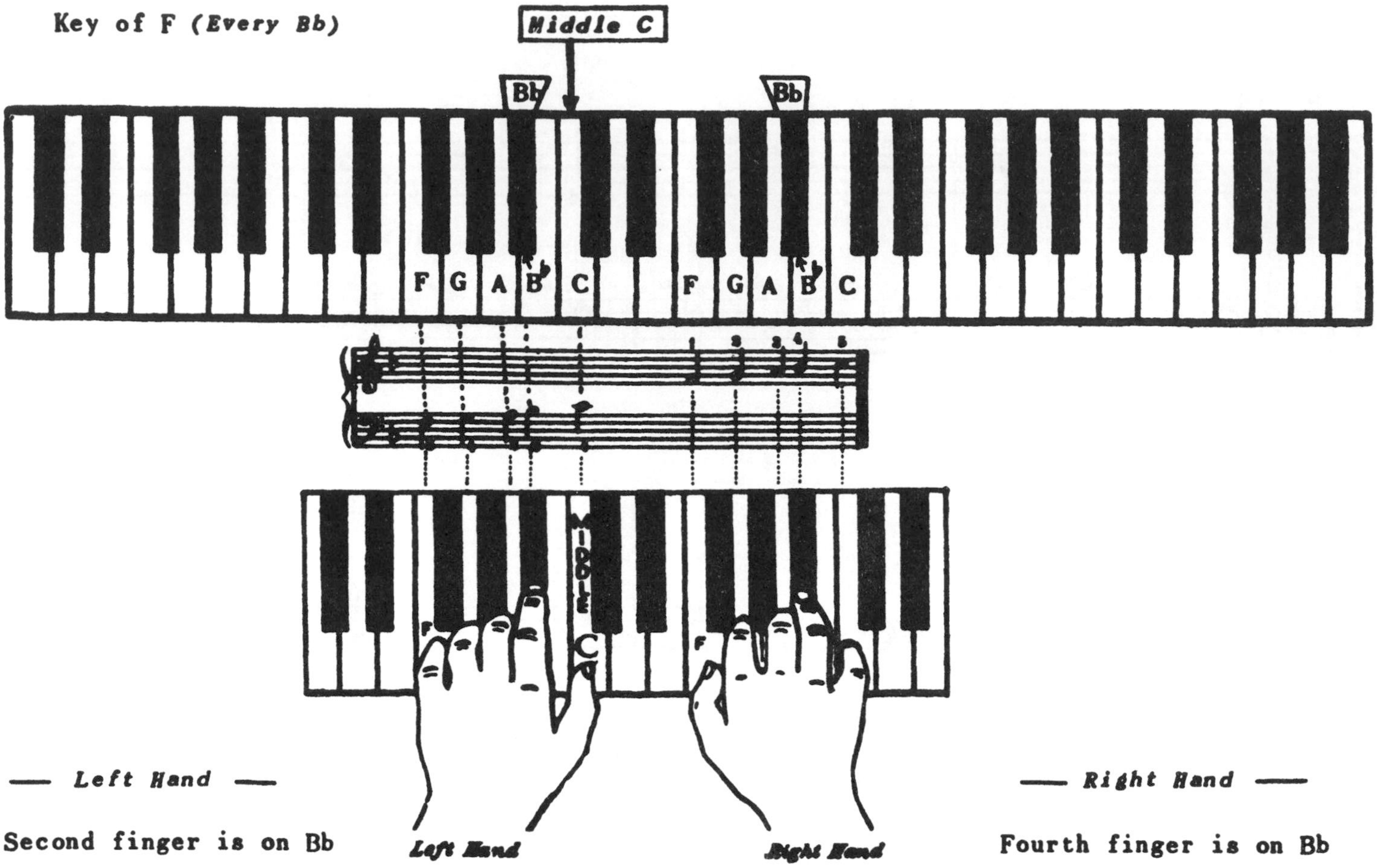

Middle C

Bb Bb

F G A Bb C F G A Bb C

— Left Hand —

Second finger is on Bb

— Right Hand —

Fourth finger is on Bb

Quarter Notes in Right Hand

1 2 3 4 5
F G A Bb C
5 4 3 2 1
F G A Bb C

Quarter Notes in Left Hand

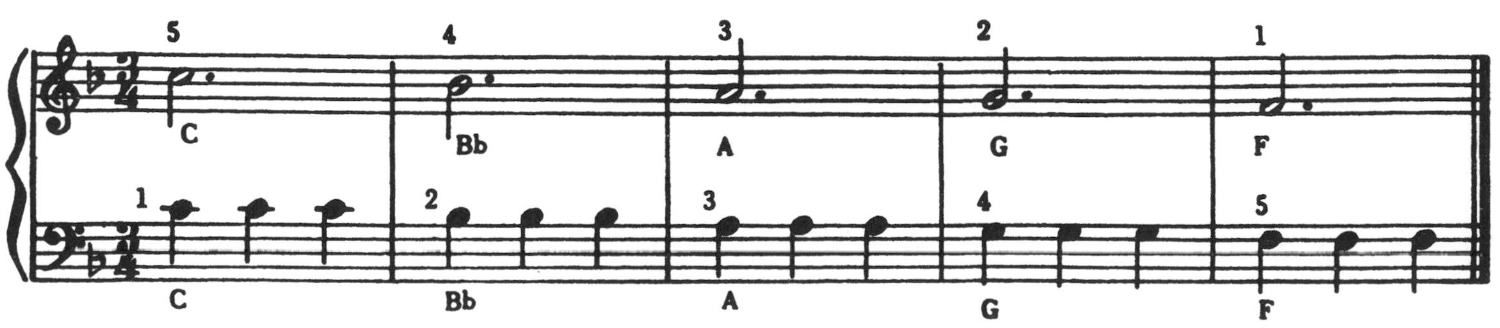
5 4 3 2 1
C Bb A G F
1 2 3 4 5
C Bb A G F

Left Hand Song in F Position

Key of F *(Every Bb)*

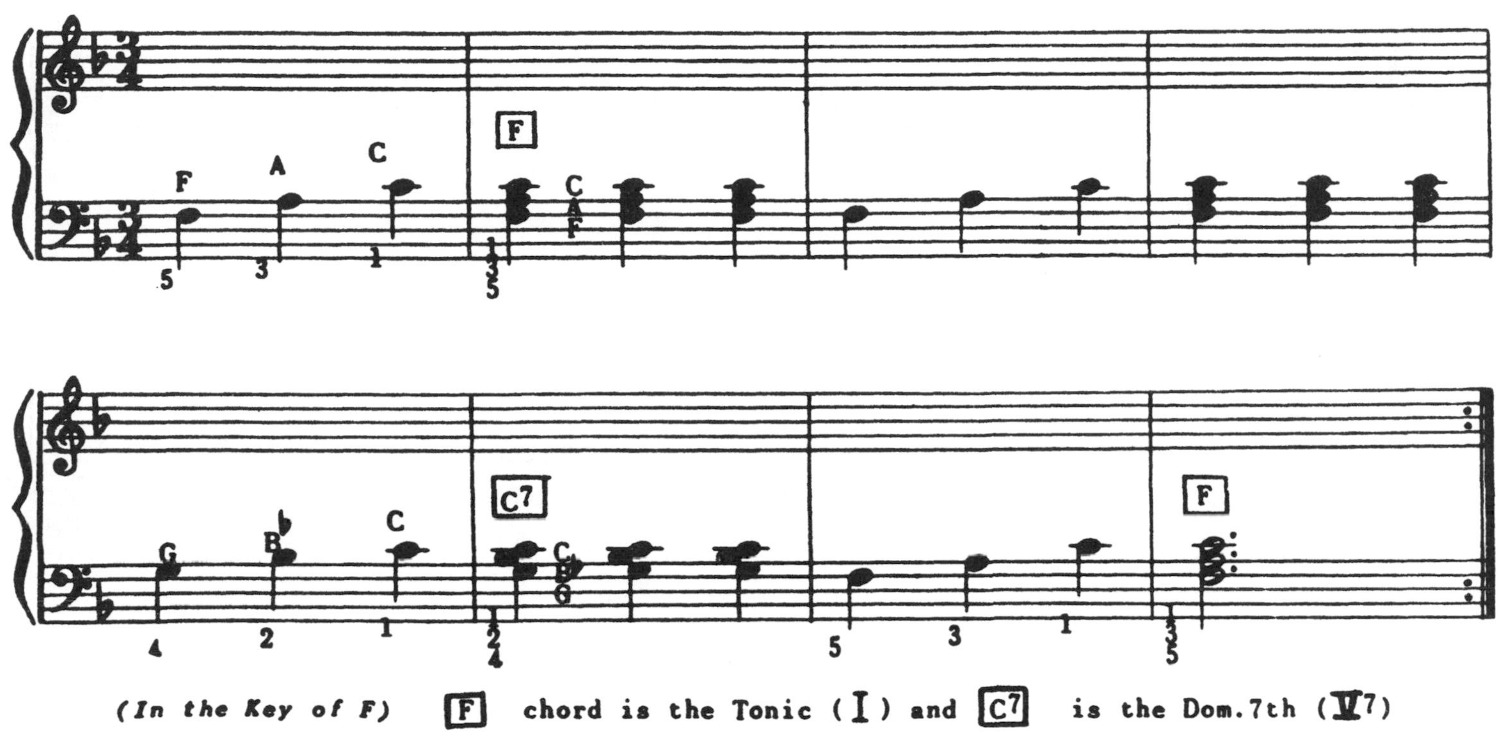
F
F
A
C
C
A
F
5
3
1
1
3
5
C7
F
G
B♭
C
C
B♭
G
4
2
1
1
2
4
5
3
1
1
3
5

(In the Key of F) F chord is the Tonic (I) and C7 is the Dom.7th (V7)

Right Hand Song in F Position

Student may write in the Letter-Names of the notes. *(Refer to P.30)*

1
3
5
5
F
1
3
5
2
4
5
5
1
3
5
5
3
1
C7
F
1
2
4
1
3
5

Sunny Skies

Andante non troppe = *Slowly, but not too much so.*

mp
Sun - ny bright skies,
And so clear blue;
What a fine day,
To be with you.
F
C7
F
C7
F
Left Hand 5th Finger Extended to E
F
C7
F
E F G A B♭ C
(5) 5 4 3 2 1

Right Hand Study

(1st Finger extends down to E.)
(E)
G

Sweet Dreams

F
mp
Sweet
Dreams my
loved
one,
(L.H. in broken chords, practise L.H. alone first)

C7
Sleep
on till
F
day - - -
light.

Sweet
Dreams my
loved
one,

C7
All
through the
F
night.

" SINGING COWBOYS " by Joseph Estella
— An excellent teaching piece that may be used at this time. —

Fun With Broken Chords

*(A Pedal Study)

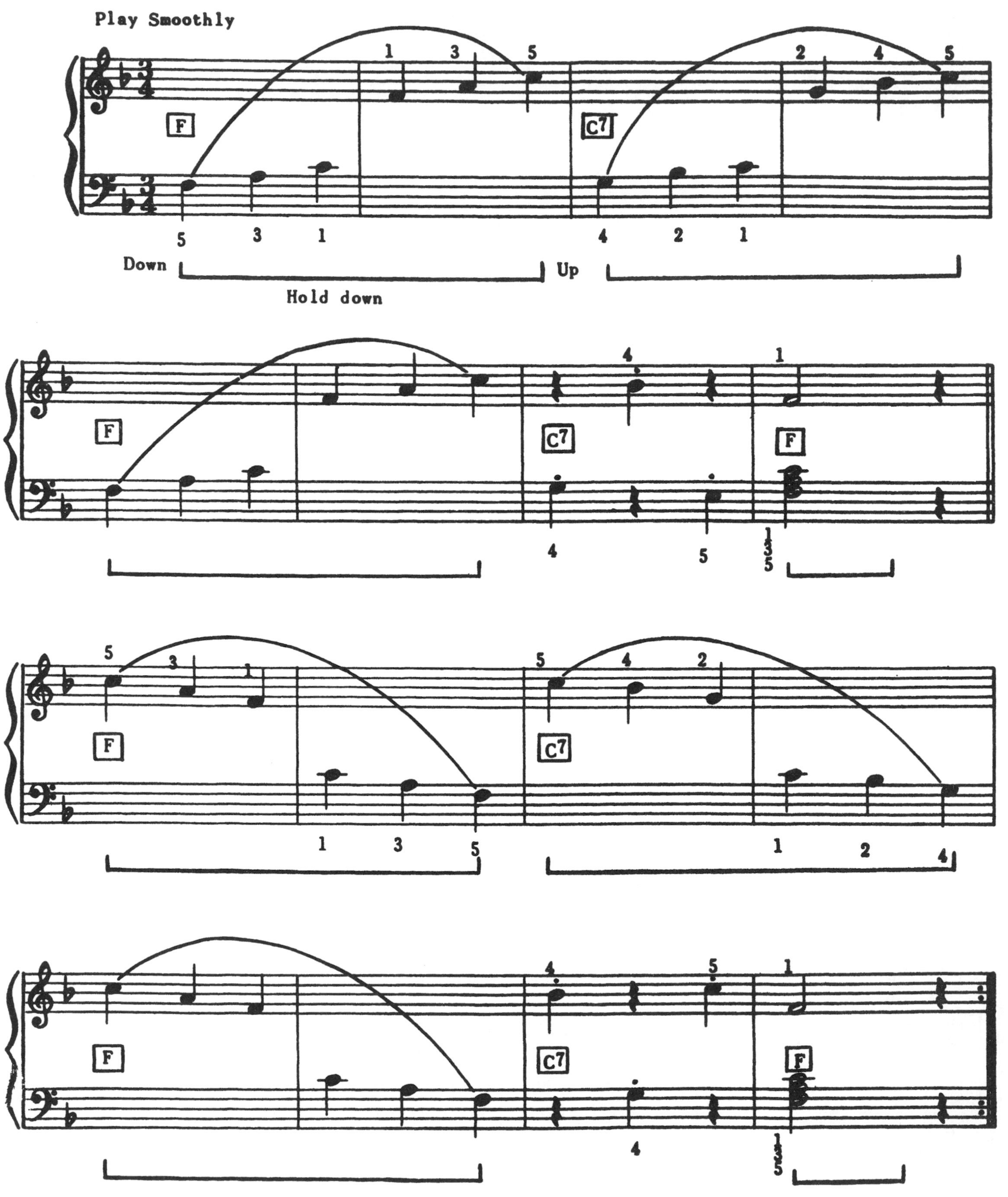
Play Smoothly
F
C7
Down
Up
Hold down

* Use the pedal to the right.

Lazy Mary
Moderato
F
mp
La - zy Ma - ry will you get up? Will
C7
you get up ? Will you get up ?
(See R.H. Study page 33)
Extend 1st down to E
Mid.C
L.H.
DOTTED LINE above indicates that the Melody shifts from the R.H. to the L.H. then back to the R.H. again.
1st back to F
F
La - zy Ma - ry will you get up ? Will
C7
F
you get up to - day ?

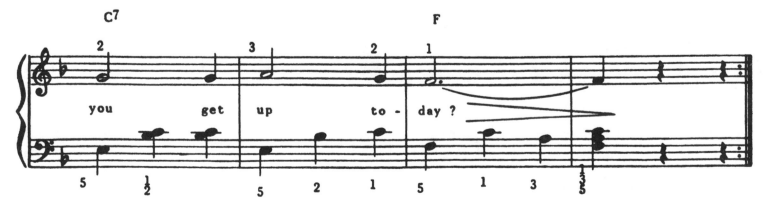

NOTE: Upon the completion of this book, you are now ready to proceed with Book Two of the "Everybody Likes the Piano" course.

FOR FUN NOW: Let's try to play America. This arrangement is in the F position with an occasional shift in the R.H. Since we have not yet had the eighth notes and dotted notes explained, it would be best to sing along with the song to help with the note values. These will be developed in the next book.

America

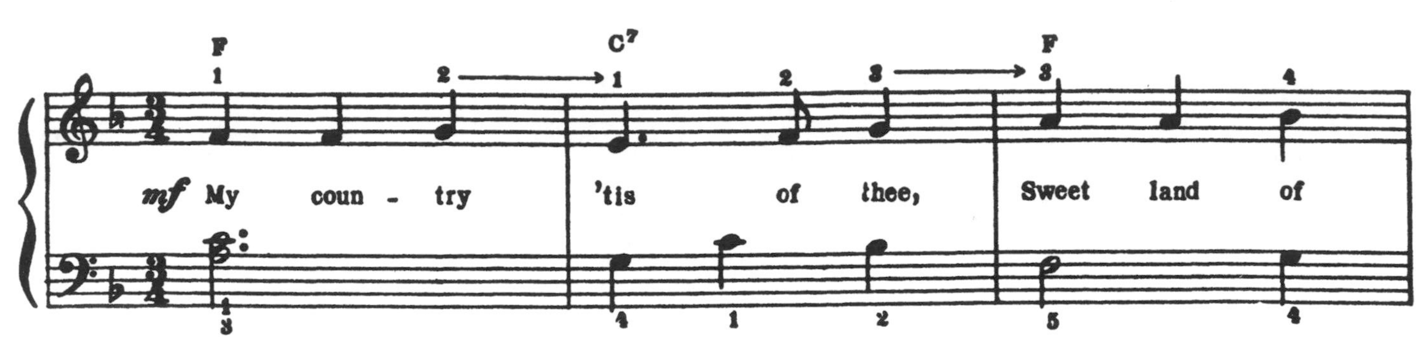
F
C7
F
mf My coun - try 'tis of thee, Sweet land of

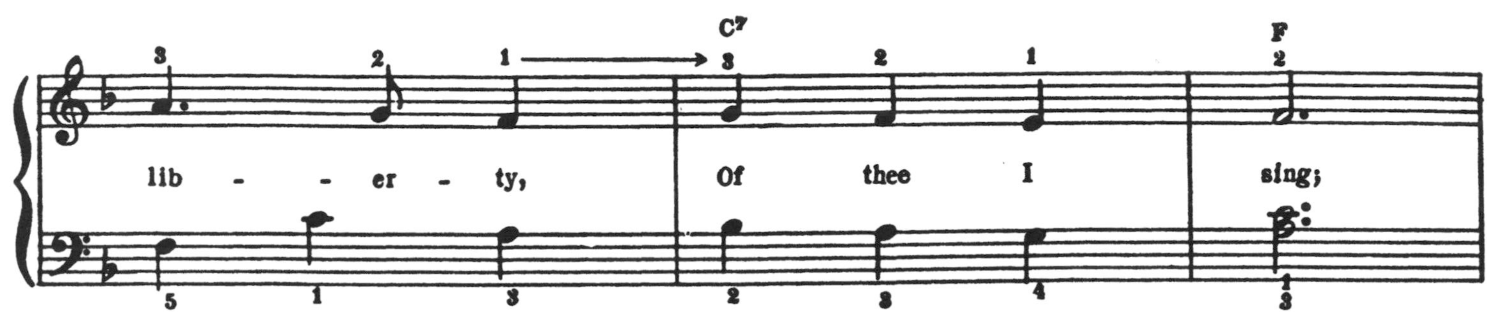
C7
F
lib - - er - ty, Of thee I sing;

F
C7
Land where my fa - ther's died, Land of the Pil - grim's pride,

F
B♭ F C7 F
From ev - 'ry moun - tain side, Let free - dom ring.

Please notice that an arrow is used to help show where R.H. shifts.